A Journal of healing and hurting

Myah Lawrence

BookLeaf Publishing

India | USA | UK

Presentation by *BookLeaf Publishing*

Web: www.bookleafpub.com

E-mail: info@bookleafpub.com

ISBN: 9789363314771

First edition 2024

*To every life experience, moment in time
and soul that has unknowingly become
interweaved with mine.*

ACKNOWLEDGEMENT

Thank you to bookleaf for the incredible opportunity, thank you to my friends and family who have supported and encouraged me and thank YOU, my readers for giving my words inquisitive minds to nestle into.

PREFACE

Within these pages, I ask that you allow these verses to be your companions through moments of solitude and celebration. Immerse yourself in the healing power of words, and let the hurting be a cathartic release.

Healing and hurting

Despite,
the correlation
of healing and time,
I have grown to understand
they aren't so easily
intwined.
For time can keep ticking,
with the absence of healing.
One second after another prolonging unpleasant
feelings;
a more accurate statement...
healing takes time.
Because time does not do the work,
as I am coming to realise.
My healing and my hurting grow simultaneously
and time is but a spectator,
that watches on curiously.

Sirens melody

The whispers
of my heart
are a sirens song
to which my redemption
and damnation
sing along.

Dance of the plight

Some people say
they have a feeling
that
their life
won't be long.
I do not have that feeling
but,
how wrong is it to want?
That way at least I know soon
there will be an end.
But how wrong is it
to slow dance with the temptation
of surrendering to death.

I survive

I'm hurting
inside;
the pain,
ever present
a sign.
I survive.
I am surviving.

Heartbreak

I thought heart break
would feel more sudden
like a glass that shatters on the floor.

It's more like seeing a glass fall
and remain intact,
seemingly unscathed from it all .

Then as you reach to pick it up;
the cracks become more evident.
You place it on the kitchen counter
aware of it now being more delicate.

For a while,
it stays there
standing on the side upright
every now and again it's cracked fragments,
catching the hues of the light.

Slowly,
a piece falls
crumbling into the glass
and another piece follows
as the slightest of breezes might pass.

Some pieces are too lost
for it now to ever be perfectly whole.
Some pieces have simply gone
they've forever been stolen.

I thought heart break;
would feel more sudden
like a glass that shatters on the floor.
Not a slow constant cracking
permeating right through my core.

Icarus

I was bathed in the glow of sun beams
when all I've ever known is starlight,
You were the warmth of day
when I was accustomed to night;
I became Icarus
in active flight
and allowed your warmth
to become my temporary delight.

Anteros

At what point
will love feel like power;
instead of weakness
the epitome of sweetness
Instead of a blade taken to my achilles;
heal,
instead of breaking.
Real,
instead of unreciprocated
I am Eros absent of Anteros.

Choose me

I have enough sense
to know I should choose myself.
It's not that my brain lacks the knowledge
it's that my heart wants something else.
No matter how aware I may be
I should not beg to be chosen.
There are multiple parts inside of me
still incredibly broken;
that is the place I draw from,
as I sit here and contemplate,
why I wasn't enough for you.
I struggle to even begin thinking straight.
Sometimes I really do wish,
I could respond with anger.
Maybe I'm too consumed by pain and hurt
for that to be my answer.
When I eventually learn
how to silence my treacherous heart,
I will have not only the sense and knowledge
but the strength,
to choose myself from the very start.

Unclaimed

I reflect on a life that is not mine
one I cannot claim as my own;
yet these memories are here
as my responsibility to disown,
if I so wish.
I lived through these times, experiences
these years
as a passenger on a freight train fuelled by fear.
I cannot claim this life as my own
when it was spent on autopilot in survival mode.

The seas side

The seas side, is where I sat.
Not quite in the sea just perched on the bank
every once in a while,
it would reach out to me.
Calling me closer, begging me not to leave,
I sat and wondered if the ocean ever felt alone
if that is why the tide comes up
when everyone goes home
Does it want a closer look into the multicoloured
houses?
Is that it's way of reminding us,
it is here when no one else is ?
As if to save me from the depths of my
complicated mind.
I heard a familiar call,
from somewhere quite close by.
Lay upon an Island of rock
peeking out of the sea,
the wide, innocent eyes of a seal, were fixated
on me.
We exchanged a knowing look, I could've
sworn I saw them smile,
My eyes did not move an inch
I stared rather beguiled.
The seal was comfy at its home,

it was time for me to find mine.
The sea watched me walk away
with the seal by its side.

Intangible

Will anyone ever hold me the way the wind
does;
caress my cheeks with as gentle a touch,
Embrace me with as much intensity in the midst
of a storm,
leave my skin tingle adorned,
Will anyone posses me, the way the wind does?

A promise

My heart will stay soft.
I promise myself.
As I patch it up,
before I reinflate it.
The air it has lost
I promise it it wasn't wasted,
it stares up at me
as I cradle it
and then it simply says;
I wasn't made to be broken
but if I stay soft
I'm easier to mend.

The sun

I think I admire the sun
it rises
no matter what comes.
When the day is grey
and clouds block it's rays
It shows up
it's there,
and that's enough.

I choose

I release myself
from the prison of guilt,
that heavy weighted quilt
of burden atop me.
I leave behind the "what if I didn't"
and the dreams for a reality that just isn't..mine.
I have to believe that what is meant for me,
will be, with the absence of cries or pleas,
I choose to believe in my journey.
I choose to know.. that I am worthy.

Self portrait

The mirror after a shower.
The mist on the car windows before you drive.
Your eyes,
holding the tear drops you so stubbornly deny.
A cloud that has fallen.
The head in-front of you at a performance.
The light;
at the end of the tunnel you peer into,
but are then made blind.
My self perception;
exists,
as a distorted reflection;
The blurred camera lens,
before it's focused,
frosted glass
on a winters night.
A self portrait would be nice,

if I knew what I looked like
or understood my own mind.
But
just as you would the mist on the car windows
before you drive;
I squint my eyes
and cannot find…
me.

So can I

They fall.
They fly.
They soar.
They cry.
We never truly wonder why; as we know it's part
of life.
So if the clouds up in the sky
can do it, so can I!
Carry such a heavy load yet
still manage to rise.

Pessimisms clutches

These thoughts ..are confusing.
Time consuming.
Ruining.
Nothing new is blooming
as the negative is choosing
to keep pursuing
the rational my brain is producing
i'm losing.
These thoughts are ruling..
over me.

Blooming

I'll write about my life
though it's hard,
with the scars
of the past on my heart.
I'm waiting for them to depart
so that I can start
something truly beautiful.

It's not as simple as it seems
because they've become me
and I realise
I don't need them to be gone
to be myself and feel free.

They've made me who I am
that now, I understand
and I'm grateful for the times
I found it hard,
I didn't know I was becoming me.
A sunflower blooming in the spring
for all to see.

Beyond goodbye

We've spent some years without you
Secretly hoping somehow you'd return to,
us.
We know it doesn't work like that
but hoping you'd somehow come back
sort of fills that empty part
of our hearts you took when you departed.
Who knew goodbye could hurt so much?
How on earth are we supposed to just
live our lives without you here?
without your hug to soothe our fears,
Your fingertips to wipe our tears,
your years,
of wisdom and love
to warm us all up
in this cold and empty world.

There's so much we have to say
to tell you since you went away
but overall we thank you
for being you and teaching us how to,
love, so hard we carry on.
You're not gone,
you're here because,
we carry a piece of you

With us everyday.
You're on repeat inside our brains.
We love you more than we can say
but you knew that anyway.

It's never actually goodbye
you left this earth
But not our lives.
We'll see you soon
until that day arrives ;
we'll carry on for you we'll thrive

Ode to poetry

I believe,
I have found my one true love
and it's the lyricism bound
upon pages of books
for which I uncage
my white doves.

Hurting and healing?

Through poetry's embrace,
wounds begin to mend.
The ink I have to face
now a lifelong friend.
I've scribbled my distress
rhyming my pain,
hearts secrets confessed
In a rhythmic refrain.
The page is now a reflection,
I've never seen myself clearer.
I've starved myself of affection
failing to be a whole hearted hearer.
So as I conceal my body and mind
within poetry's embrace.
I allow myself the time
to learn to extend myself the same grace.